AF323234

# REDUNDANCIES, AGAIN!

Especially for you!
From
Susie Andruk

Hope you enjoy "each
and every" one of our
redundancies "all "collected
together."
Best regards,
David O'Connor

# Redundancies, Again!

**By
David O'Connor
and
Susie Andruk**

Illustrated by Susie Andruk

*Exposition Press       Smithtown, New York*

*To Lisa, Michela, Greg, and Nancy*

**redundancy:**
- the quality or state of being redundant: superfluity;
- profusion, overabundance;
- superfluous repetition: an act or instance of needless repetition;
- the part of the message that can be eliminated without loss of essential information

# Contents

# Preface

It is true that nothing should be done without purpose. With this in mind, some people may ponder the purpose of assembling redundancies of the English language into a volume such as this. It is not merely a salutary exercise, but an attempt to humorously draw attention to the verbosities to which we are subjected each day. In *Oracles of Nostradamus* (1891), C. A. Ward commented on redundancy. He stated that "a plethora of words becomes the apoplexy of reason." In the near-century since this statement, man has continued to hastily fit too many words to a single thought. By bringing attention to the redundancy, we wish to encourage others to make every word count, for surely simplicity is the most difficult achievement of style!

# Redundancies, Again!

# 1

# Trite and Common Errors of the Tongue

Each and every one

Extra bonus

Free gift

Free gratis

Over and above

Good benefits

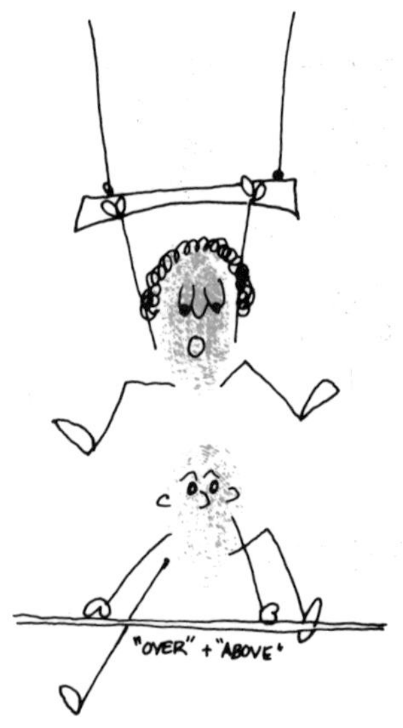


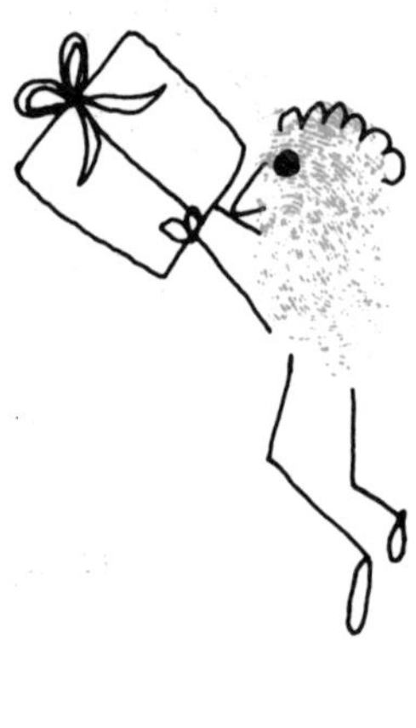

Please R.S.V.P.
    (brought to our attention by Mike Hayes)

"Reinforce again"—Mari Nuckles

Now in progress

Advance planning

Planning ahead

Mental telepathy

Positive mental attitude
   (called to our attention by Bill Miller)

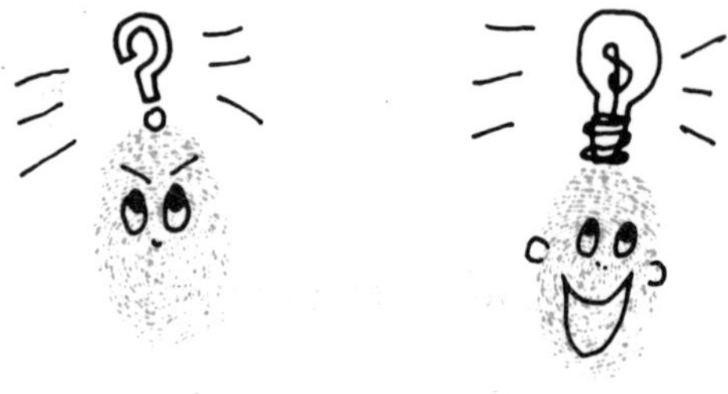

# 2

# Politics and Other Double Talk

I would first like to preface my opening remarks with
this preamble.

"The future lies ahead"—Goodwin Knight, former governor of California

"He made the wrong mistake"—George Bush, quoting Yogi Berra

"Convincingly persuasive"—Jimmy Carter, President

"Sole single purpose"—Gerald Ford

"Widely used, worldwide"—Kiara Kritz

"Liberally and freely"—J. B. Nethercutt

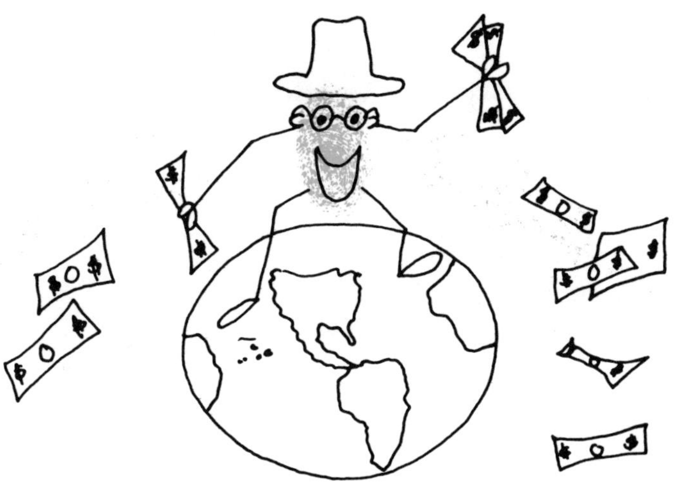

"Trade-offs, back and forth"—Mike Hayes

Vacillate back and forth

"Influential in influencing"—Jack Heidt, president of Union Bank

"Relevant relevance"—Victor Cole, president, Cole, Green, and Associates

"Lasting, long-term results"—Vince Caracio, president, Sales Techniques

"A causeway of human humanity"—Harry Reasoner

"Export out"—Jack Heidt

"Expedite your order faster"—Roberta Bolinsky

"Best solution that will solve the problem"—David O'Connor

"Successful formulas that work"—David Soul

"A big major problem"—Barbara Kenton

"Unsolved problems"—Susan England

"Puzzling riddles"—KPOL Radio

"Knowledge of knowing the answer"—Dick Nolind

$$4\left(\frac{x+y^2}{\sqrt{6}} + z^4 \times (\pi+3)\right) - 7 \geq ?$$

Present incumbent

Other alternative

Qualified expert

Proficient competency

"First time back in competitive competition"—Frank
  Gifford

"Necessary ingredients that are mandatory"—KPOL
   Radio

"New additions to the list"—Marilyn Acton

Complete monopoly

"Long-shot gamble"—Bob Seager

"Preparation ahead of time"—Marlene Gerloff

*procrastination*: to postpone until later

"Behind in back taxes"—"Hawaii Five-O"

# Consensus of opinion

# Current popular trend

Essential necessity

Very extremely definite

"Important and urgent"—president, Hospital Council
of Southern California

"Emergency problems"—Ken Potokar

"A safe haven"—"60 Minutes"

True facts

The honest truth

# Opponents against the bill

# 3

# Groupies and Loners

Assemble together

Join together

Merged together

"Group items together"—Roberta Bolinsky

"Collectively together"—Roberta Bolinsky

"Pair off in couples, two by two"—John Danley

"Combining the two together"—Monica Hollister

"Tied all together in one package"—Monica Hollister

"A basket of 25 donut holes in a basket for $1.25"
   —a sign in Yum Yum Donut Store

"Pairs of two"—Bob Cordell

The two twins

A pair of tiny dwarf twins

Perpetual generations keep repeating themselves

"The mother of children"—Debby Albrecth

"Is he still married to his wife?"—Greg Andruk

"I'm going to have a boy brother"—Nancy Andruk,
    age 3

One lone dancer

"Separately alone"—Roberta Bolinsky

"Nine separate different ones"—Mike Hayes

"Can carry itself on its own"—Mike Hayes

"Single individual"—Kenny Rogers

"Totally different and unique"—Marlene Gerloff

"One single most important thing"—David O'Connor

Widow woman

Widow of the late . . .

"One parrot bird"—Nancy Andruk, age 3

"25¢ for each additional passenger more than one"
(seen in a Texas taxi)

"Lost their last eleven games in a row"—Mike Hayes

"Own personal investment"—Lou LaMair

# 4

# Dubious Delinquents

"With one shot, we'll get them all at once!"—Mike Hayes

"Fatally killed"—Connie O'Kelley

"Total, quick, and complete death"—*Handbook of Consumer Motivation*

"Threatening him with an assassination threat" —Barbara Walters to Richard Nixon regarding Spiro Agnew

"This guy jumped off the Saint Paul Bridge and committed suicide and died."—Dielle Sabin

Temporarily suspended because he was not warned
  beforehand

"In trouble? Lift your hood up."
  ( seen on the Santa Monica Freeway, by Cal Trans )

"Malicious vandalism"—Mike Hayes

"Disappears from sight"—Susie Andruk

"Prisoners in jail"—David Sandberg

# 5

## Sensory Perceptions and Other Body References

"Stark naked and totally nude"—Mike Hayes

"Bare naked"—Susan England

Natural instincts

Human being

"Human person"—George Fencer

Sang a vocal solo

Speaks with a slow drawl

"Verbose at the mouth"—Susie Andruk


Stand up on your feet

Foot pedal

"Pedestrian foot traffic"—Frank Parziale

"See with your very own eyes"—"The Electric
   Company"

"Visually, it is difficult to look at."—Susie Andruk

Clearly visible to the eye

Smooth feeling in texture

# 6

# Where It's At

Brought to our attention by Sidney Brownell:

Advance forward

Proceeded on

Close proximity

Revert back

Refer back

Continue on

End result

"Empty void"—Pat Allomong

Highest summit

Ascend upward

"Escalate up"—Gene Morris

"Pouring down"—Gary Hollister

"Descend down"—Pamela McGinnis, KMPC Radio

"Deep down"—Dielle Sabin

Downstairs basement

Underground tunnel

"Stacked vertically"—Stuart Papell

"Squashed flat"—Dave DeSoto, KMPC Radio

Penetrating in

Outdoor outings

Point of destination

"Walked in from the entrance doors"—J. B.
    Nethercutt

"Far, opposite end"—David M. O'Connor

Cross over the bridge . . .

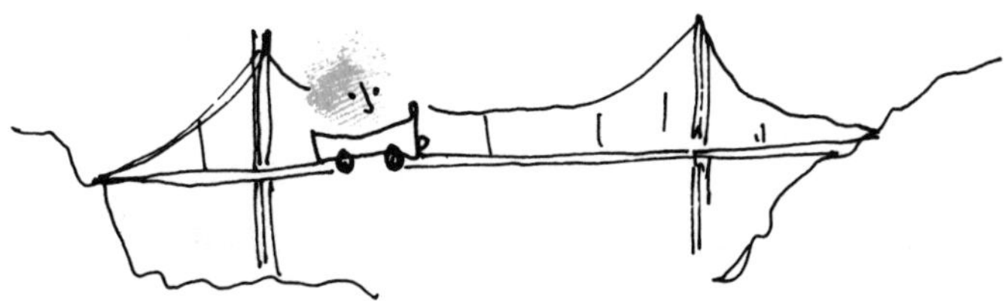

. . . to the suburbs of the city

# 7

# Mathematical and Mechanical Misnomers

From Stuart Papell:

"Round circle"

"Perfect square"

"Rectangular in shape"

And from Gene Morris:

"Pinnacle point"

Mechanical robot

Automated self-moving toys

"Repetitive design that's done all over"—Terry Storms

Five in number

"Consistent, same size"—Sidney England

# 8

# Hot Ones!

Burns up

Fiery holocaust

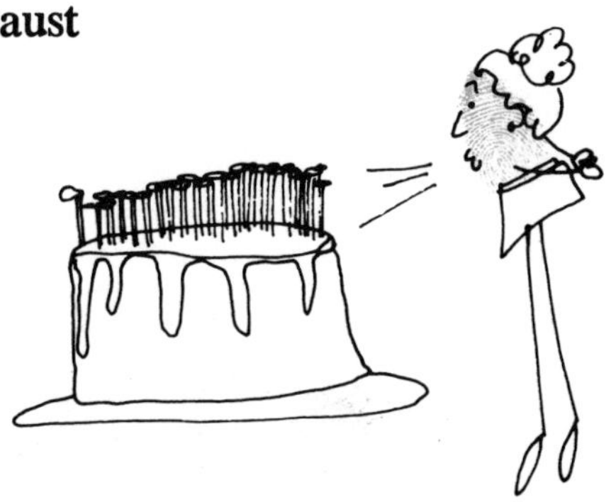

Summer season

Heats up

Hot-water heater

# 9

# Literary and Artistic Contributions

An exact copy

"Reduplicate again"—Gena Selmont

"A display exhibit"—David M. O'Connor

Forwarding preface

"Pre-anticipate"—Walt DeLorrell

# Matinee in the afternoon

*As a Youngster in My Youth: An Autobiography of Myself*, by Jack Evans

*My Autobiography*, by Charlie Chaplin

The same identical stories

Biography of his life

Complete unabridged edition

Melody Tune (that's her name!)

"Nationally the #1 song all over the country"—KNX
  Radio

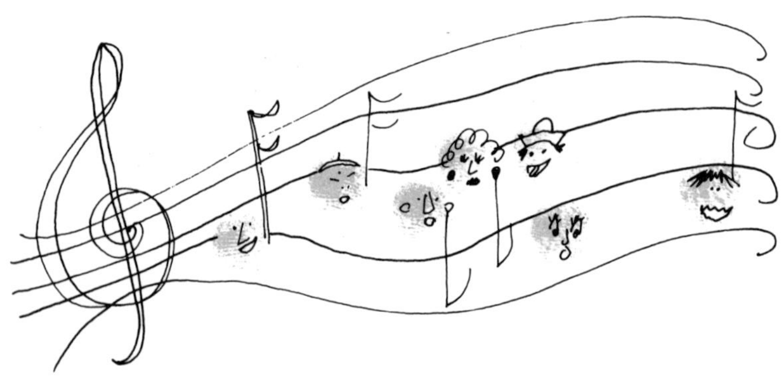

# 10

## Something Old, Something New, Something Borrowed, Something Blue...

SOMETHING OLD...

"Past history: old legends, old adages"—Mari Nuckles

Old antiques:
    Restored again
    Exact replica

"Previously, for the past forty-five years"—Gary Hollister

"I remember recalling"—Darlene Moan

SOMETHING NEW . . .

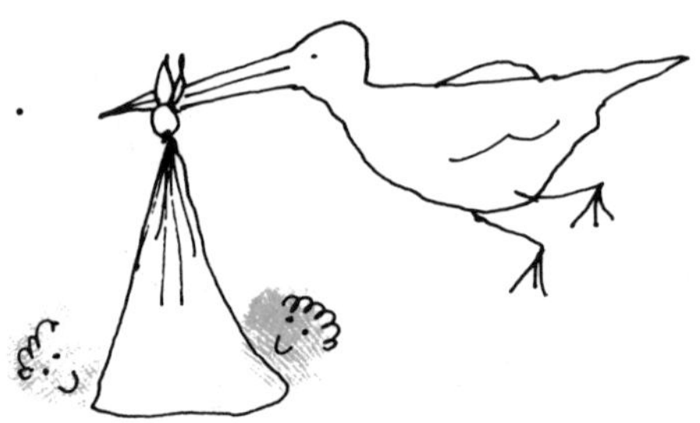

First introduction

Initial start

New innovation

"New, updated image"—Roberta Bolinsky

"Project forward into the future"—Arthur O. Armstrong

"Looking forward to the future with great anticipation"—Georgene Jackson

"Predict ahead of time"—Stuart Papell

"Preamble before we start"—Hilary Farnell

"Final conclusion"

"Final result"

. . . and from Marti Morrisey:

"Revacuum again"

Blue in color

# 11

# Miscellaneous Pleonasms



"Rich millionaire"—Peggy Swanson

"Young teenage adolescent"—Peggy Swanson

"My dean who is the dean of students"—Elsie Bruno

"An hour of time"—Donna James

"10:00 P.M. at night"—Dielle Sabin

"It stayed light the whole time before it got dark"—
Ken Potokar

Once-a-year winter sale

"Twice a year, once every six months"—Monica
Hollister

Ongoing, continuing

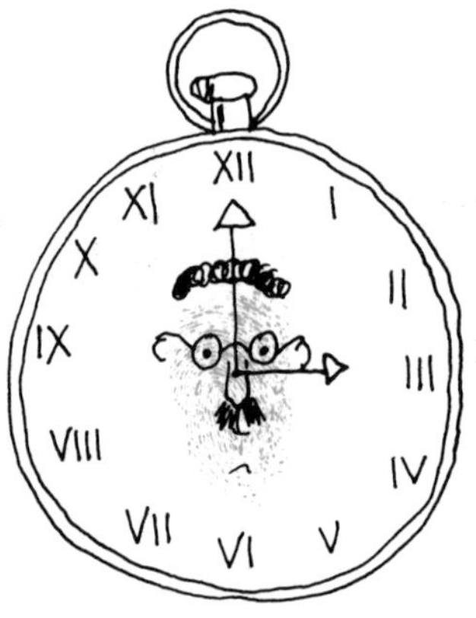

"Annual sales for the year"—Karen Bradley

"Open 7 days a week, including Sunday"—Dielle Sabin

"Repeated your employment again"—Merv Griffin

"Free advertising that you don't have to pay for"—
  Hilary Farnell

"The goal of advertising is = profit"—Hilary Farnell

"Foreign import"—KNX Radio

"Factory rebate from the factory"—Cal Worthington

"Superbowl game"—Laurie Jackson

From Jim McKay during the Winter Olympics of
1980:

"The precise same moment"

"Dominance by the Russians is expected to be
thorough, complete, and total"

"Genuine precious stones"—Star of Siam commercial

"It not only serves as a freshener, it freshens your makeup"—Mary Anne O'Rourke

"Alternate cleansers are quicker and faster to use" —Vicki E. Wilson

"A purse-size for your purse"—Hilary Farnell

"Keep in a cool, dark place away from the light" —Virginia Coe

"Dissolves away"—Alice Nichols

"If they melt, they'll thaw out"—Gena Selmont

"So what, who cares . . . ?"—Cathy Davis (and prob-
ably the rest of the world!)